T0132308

Boy or Girl? Man or Woman?

Children, know the truth!

ABBA'S SERVANT

Order this book online at www.trafford.com
or email orders@trafford.com

Most Trafford titles are also available at major online book retailers.

 www.trafford.com

North America & international
toll-free: 844 688 6899 (USA & Canada)
fax: 812 355 4082

Our mission is to efficiently provide the world's finest, most comprehensive book publishing service, enabling every author to experience success. To find out how to publish your book, your way, and have it available worldwide, visit us online at www.trafford.com

ISBN: 978-1-6987-1535-3 (sc)
ISBN: 978-1-6987-1536-0 (e)

Library of Congress Control Number: 2023917491

Print information available on the last page.

Trafford rev. 09/15/2023

CHILDREN,

Know the truth...

Same sex relationships are not ...

ABBA'S SERVANT

Children, you were born because of a male and a female. If it were not for a man and a woman coming together, you would not exist. So, for someone to teach you that a man and a man or that a woman and a woman are husband and wife is the biggest lie that has been taught to you.

The Lord and God of all the earth declares that He made them" male and female". Jesus Lord and Savior of all that call upon Him answered and said unto them, (Matthew 19:4-6) Have you not read, that He which made them at the beginning made them male and female, and said, For this cause shall a man leave father and mother, and shall cleave to his wife: and they twain shall be one flesh? Wherefore they are no more twain, but one flesh. What therefore God hath joined together, let not man put asunder.

Look! You can see this truth for yourself. Male and female joined together-becomes one- one flesh. There is no other way to become ONE FLESH except when a male and female date each other or there is a marriage between them. What joins them together is the connection of their different body parts. And when those parts fall into the right position, man and woman are one.

"Leave father and mother." And cleave unto his wife.
How shall this be without a male and a female?

Make no mistake about this, Children, there is a God who owns the heavens and the earth and all that is therein. In the Bible, Moses told the people in Deuteronomy 30:19—20, that I call heaven and earth to record this day against you, that I have set before you life and death, blessing and cursing, therefore choose life, that both thou and thou seed may live: that thou mayest love the LORD thy God, and that thou mayest obey His voice, and that thou mayest cleave unto Him: for He is thy life. In the New Testament, Jesus spoke, John 3:16, For God so loved the world, that He gave His only begotten Son, that whosoever believeth in Him should not perish, but have everlasting life. For God sent not His Son into the world to condemn the world; but that the world through Him might be saved. He that believeth on Him is not condemned: but he that believeth not is condemned already, because he hath not believed in the name of the only begotten Son of God.

Make no mistake about this: it does not matter if you believe the Bible or do not believe in God.

The day is coming when you will.

People are living on feelings rather than truth. The truth is what you don't see has made what you now see.

No one sees the baby the moment the Male sperm connects with the Female egg, but something begins to develop. It is like planting a bean seed. You put a seed in a cup of soil, water it, give it sunlight, and a few weeks later up pops a sprout.

"Males don't have eggs and females don't have sperm."

Children, don't you know that there is an opposite for ALL most ALL THINGS? The number line has positive and negative numbers except for zero. There is no match for the zero. There is no match to the One and True Living

God. He is God the Father, God the Son, and God the Holy Ghost. Together, they make One.

There is no match for Them.

You have a left foot and right foot unless for some unfortunate mishap there are some people who have neither. Why do you think shoemakers make shoes for the left foot and one for the right foot? The feet are designed differently. So, people make items for the right side of the body and for the left side of the body.

Your eyes, your hands, your ears, and your nose.

Why do you think you have only one brain? It is because you only need one to control your body, but there are two sides of the brain to control each side of your body.

That is why same sex attraction is not of God. It is of the devil. A square peg will never fit into a triangle peg's space.

I am using all these analogies to get the point across. A boy, man, or male will never be a female. They may cut off, sew on but in the end, they are still not a girl, a woman, or female. Even though they changed their looks and some body parts, the original body will always be male. Same for females. A girl, woman, or female will never be a male. Even though they may change their looks, cut off some body parts, and add some body parts, the original body will always be female.

"Females skeletons are different than the male skeletons."

God has that 'I change not." So how on earth does a child, man, woman, or parent get to change the gender of what he or she was born?

They do not get this option. Romans chapter 1: 20 explains why humans try to change their natural sex organs to the opposite.

Ever since God made the world, He has been showing people clearly about Himself. We cannot see God, but the things that He has made show us clearly, what He is like. We can understand His great power that continues forever. We can know that He is the true God. So, there is no reason for anyone to say, "We could not know about God."

In the Bible it talks about the people of the Old Testament. Romans 1:21-28 it states that those people really knew about God, but they did not respect Him as a great God, and they did not thank Him. They did not even think clearly anymore. Their minds became confused and they did not understand God's message. They said that they were wise, but really they became fools. They refused to worship the great God who can never die. Instead, they made false gods for themselves. They worshipped idols that were like people who must die. They also made idols that looked like birds, animals, and snakes, and they worshipped them. So, God let those people do all the bad things that they wanted to do. God let those disgusting things rule their lives.

As a result, they did bad things with each other's bodies. They did things that people should be ashamed to do. They refused to believe the true things about God. Instead, they chose to believe lies. They worshipped things that God has made and they became servants of those things. But they refused to worship God Himself who made those things! Everyone should praise Him forever! Amen.

This is true. Because those people turned against God, He let those band things rule their lives. They strongly wanted to do things that they should be ashamed about. Even the women stopped having sex in a way which is proper. Instead, they began to have sex with other women, which is not proper.

Also, the men stopped having sex with women.

Instead, they strongly wanted to have sex with other men. Men did bad things with other men that they should be ashamed about. Because they did such wrong things, they received in their won bodies the punishment that was right.

Those people decided that they did not need to know anything about God. So, God let their minds become spoiled. As a result, they do bad things that people ought not to do.

This is evident today. How are parents changing the gender of their babies without consequences? They are not. Every child whose parents have altered their gender are suffering, having mixed feelings about what gender they are.

Children, if you are being told you can be another gender then you are being blindly led to a life of destruction. In Matthew 15:14, Jesus stated that if the blind lead the blind, both shall fall into the ditch.

Children, you are supposed to be trained up in the way you should go (Proverbs 22:6). As for as how you got on this earth is plain enough to train you in the way of what makes a boy a boy and a girl a girl. Children, again I say to you that you were born because a man and a woman joined their different organs.

Children, for a boy to be born a son to his mother and say he is a girl makes no sense. To do so suggests that his mother is not his mother and his father or the man whose sperm help create him is not his father or sperm donor or for a girl to say she is her mother's son and no longer her daughter. This is changing the order of life. Males cannot become pregnant, and females cannot impregnant another female.

So, why are people teaching you to think wrong.

Adults should know the if a child is born with certain organs, that child is that gender. They have chosen to believe a lie and are making their choice for sexual gender based on feelings and emotions rather than the TRUTH. The TRUTH IS THE WORD OF GOD.

Also telling you or some other child, if you feel like a girl but have a boy's body or feel like a boy and have a girl's body, you are probably the other gender. You are not the other gender, you are the gender God in Jesus created you to be (male or female). These people's minds are smeared by lies from the devil.

These people who are telling and allowing others to tell you that you or any other child can be a different gender is not the TRUTH.

CHILDREN, a man in all his effort to change his body into a female has already failed to become a female because his skeleton body structure and internal organ structure comes from the original male template created by God in Jesus. Too, a woman in all her effort to disguise her body as a male has already failed because her skeleton body structure and internal organ structure comes from the original female template created by God in Jesus. Anything added to or taken away from His creation is an abomination (Leviticus 18:22 and Revelation 21:8).

Children, the same thing that happened to the people in the world before now will happen to those who continue to practice same sex relationships and to those who continue to support same sex relationships. God destroyed Sodom (Genesis 19: because of the wickedness.

The men were having sex with men and women with women.

Children, all sexual diseases are rooted in the wicked sexual practice of people. Remember Romans, the men received the punishment that was right. Love the person but hate the sin.

Sinning sexually is against what God created brings punishment. In the beginning He created them male and female. But I would have you know, that the head of every man is Christ; and the head of the woman is the man; and the head of Christ is God (1Corthintains 11:3).

Children, gay is not the way. The letters stand for "Going against Yahweh". Yahweh is the Hebrew Name of God Almighty. For anyone choosing to come himself or herself a homosexual in relation to being lesbian, gay, bisexual, transgender, or queer, are going against the family created by Yahweh, the Living God.

Children, I write unto that you may know the truth. The truth is that God formed male and female. Let heaven and the earth be your witness. Colossians 1:16, Who is the image of the invisible God, the firstborn of every creature. For by Him were all things created, that are in heaven, and that are in earth, visible and invisible, whether they be thrones, or dominions, or principalities, or powers: all things were created by Him and for Him: and He is before all things, and by Him all things consist. God in Jeremiah 1:1 told the prophet that before He formed him in the womb He knew him, before he was born He set him apart.

God in Jesus knows the sex of a child before he or she is formed. In Psalm 139:15-16, David stated that his substance was not hid from God,

When he was made in secret, and curiously wrought in the lowest parts of the earth. God's eyes did see his substance, yet being imperfect;

And in Your book all my members were written, Which in continuance were fashioned, When as yet there was none of them.

Children, these two witnesses talk about how their bodies were formed from what the human eye cannot see -- an egg of a woman joining with a sperm of a man. Yet, they declare that God saw it happen. God saw them grow inside the bodies of their mothers.

Children, humans may alter the gender of males and females formed by God in Jesus, but this alteration will not undo what He already formed.

The male and female bodies are created differently. It is known that after a body has deteriorated and only the bones are left that the gender of the skeleton can still be determined by its bone structure.

Children, observe the following illustration and photos.

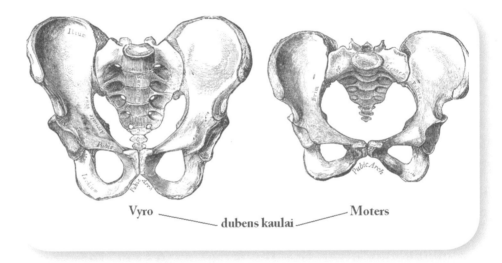

Two pelvises with drastically exaggerated differences—a man's shown on the left and a woman's on the right (identified in Lithuanian)—illustrate how sex was estimated skeletally in the early 1900s.

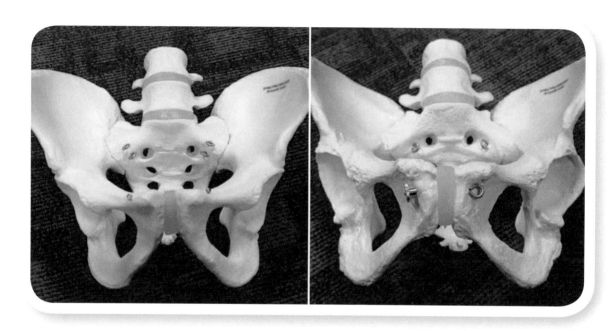

The opening that can be seen in this pelvic bone is called the pelvic inlet. If you can observe, these two pelvic bones have a different shape and size. The one on the left has a more heart shape and the pelvic inlet is smaller whereas the one on the right had a rounder shape and the pelvic inlet is bigger. The one on the left belongs to a male and the one on the right belongs to female. The reason why the female pelvic is rounder and bigger is to enable the process of childbirth.

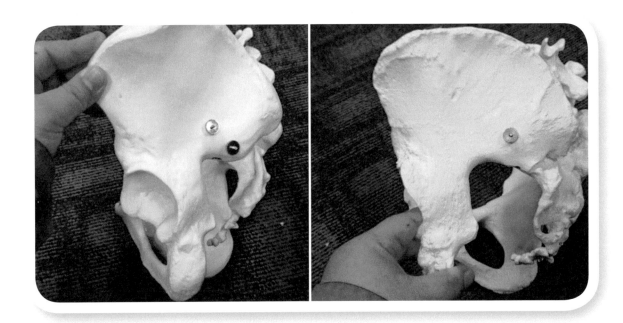

Another factor to consider while determining the sex of the person is by looking at the sciatic notch at the pelvic bone. This can be done by looking at the sides of a pelvic bone and observing the angle as shown in the diagram above. A wider sciatic notch usually means that the skeleton remains belong to a female and a narrower sciatic notch indicates that the skeleton remains belong to a male. By observing the pictures above, can you determine which pelvic bone belongs to a male and which one belongs to a female?

Children, men do not have wombs for childbearing. The TRUTH, transgenders will never be females or males. Homosexuals, gays, lesbians, queers, bisexuals are not of truth.

God in Jesus creates babies to be the gender He formed in the womb of the mother before birth.

God through Jesus before the foundation of the earth planned a life to prosper those who of us who chooses to follow Him by choosing Jesus Christ as their Lord and Savior. In John 14:6 it says, I am the way, the truth, and the life: no man cometh unto the Father, but by Me.

Only God in Jesus by His Spirit will give the peaceful and loving life desired while on this earth.

Children, only the truth will make you free from the lies that are being told to you or others about gender identity (John 8:32). Turn your situation over to Him and He through Jesus will make you free of whatever you are battling in this world.

God through Jesus loves us all and desires that all might be saved. He will only save those who comes to Him through Jesus. God will never change. He gives us the power to choose Him or satan. God will never change His Word (Jesus is the Word) for anyone. Jesus Christ the same yesterday, and to day, and for ever (Hebrews 13:8). We are the ones who must change our thinking about everything in this world that is going against His truth.

**I pray the Father in Jesus's Name by His Spirit
open your eyes to His truth. Amen.**

Printed in the United States
by Baker & Taylor Publisher Services